EARTH GIANT TREE GIFT SERIES – BOOK 8

Moreton Bay Fig's Gift

ROCHELLE HEVEREN

 TREE VOICE PUBLISHING

Earth Giant Tree Gift Series: Moreton Bay Fig's Gift

TREE VOICE PUBLISHING PTY LTD
ACN. 627 784 294 ABN . 94627784294
4 Wirreanda Court Blackburn Victoria 3130 AUSTRALIA
Phone +613 9878 4600
Email: hello@treevoice.global
www.treevoice.global

First published in 2019
Copyright text © Rochelle Heveren
Copyright © Tree Voice Publishing

www.facebook.com/TreeVoiceAuthor
www.facebook.com/RochelleHeverenAuthor
Instagram: @treevoiceglobal
Instagram: @rochelle_with_love_x

All rights reserved. No part of this publication may be reproduced in whole or in part, stored in a retrievable system, or transmitted in any form or by any means, electronic, mechanical, photocopying, recording or otherwise, without written permission of the copyright holder or publisher.

Designed by Tree Voice Publishing Pty Ltd
Printed by Ingram Spark
ISBN: 978-0-6483913-3-3 (paperback)

 A catalogue record for this book is available from the National Library of Australia

*I know with my whole being,
that when I sit and a tree connects,
that it is never just for me.*

*This little book
has BIG heart and soul.*

*My commitment to share this with you,
my friend, is promised.*

– Love Rochelle xxx

Sitting at the base of my new friend Moreton Bay Fig in the Hinterland of Queensland, Australia I feel calm stillness and love. I begin to dream...

I feel encouraged to live my life with a newfound essence. This immediately dissolves my pain, hurts and trapped mind. Dreams allow my heart to hold completeness and my body to be free from all that has held it captive. I discover the moment between a dream and its reality, the space between heaven and earth.

Foreword

Moreton Bay Fig's Gift is the channelled teachings of one of Earth's great Masters. This ancient tree, over thousands of years old, will bring you calm, love and a chance to witness the 'moment' between all things. Moreton Bay Fig holds the magic to plant seeds full of your dreams and wishes. These can then grow into your reality. You will be gifted a with unique sense of guidance on your own life's journey, reminding you of the importance of your own essence in all areas of your life. You will discover that when your own essence is washed through the hurt and pain of your life, your heart can hold completeness and be freed to love and be loved. Experience stillness, calm and be taken inward towards your own uniqueness while connecting into Moreton Bay Fig.

Being supported with the magic of *Moreton Bay Fig's Gift* is like resting your back against her trunk and listening to her whispers of great wisdom. Allow her words to encourage you with love.

This inspiring gift book is designed to unlock your own heart's wisdom. Rochelle invites you to discover the magic, stillness, newfound love and freedom that she experienced, sitting and resting her back against the Moreton Bay Fig in the Hinterland of Queensland, Australia.

Written in Queensland, Australia

Contents

Introduction 1

Chapter 1: Finding Magic 5

Chapter 2: Heart's Connection 10

Chapter 3: Dreaming 14

Chapter 4: Re-birth 19

Chapter 5: My Essence of Healing 23

Chapter 6: A Wish 26

Chapter 7: Transparency of Thought 33

Chapter 8: Changing Old Habits 37

Chapter 9: Accepting Authenticity 40

Chapter 10: The Magic of In-Between 46

Chapter 11: Imagination 50

Introduction

Knotted thoughts twist and turn in my mind. I repeatedly try to disconnect from my mixed-up, dysfunctional past. People, places and events pop up in my thoughts and then hold my mind captive. Enough! I muster much effort to free myself from the many haunting words rattling around in my mind.

Several weeks ago a chapter in my life finally ended, after many years of seeking closure. My brother now sits in a prison cell awaiting sentencing. Meanwhile, on the outside, some of his victims are captive to the pain of the past – innocent minds held for ransom, without peace or freedom. I too find myself slipping into the space of wasted thoughts, feelings and way of being, even though I know it no longer serves me to do so. How I wish I could change my programmed thoughts and move towards freedom!

This chapter of my past continues to play on in my mind, even though it has been slammed shut. My body, heart and soul have given up the story, but my mind still holds the narrative.

I lie in bed in a hotel room, resting before we drive to our final destination in the Moreton Bay region of Queensland, Australia. This trip has been planned at the last minute to try to help us finish a very busy year quietly; hopefully we can finally relax.

In total, I have 17 hours of travel time to just think.

I believe the time has come for something new, fresh and exciting to enter my world. My thoughts crave something more.

Today, as we travel toward white beaches and turquoise waters, I finally feel myself beginning to relax.

When I arrive at our booked accommodation I feel the magic of the Moreton Bay area. Most of the streets surrounding the house are lined with Illawarra flame trees, bursting with bright red flowers. Next to our lunch spot on the first day is a massive Jacaranda tree. Stunning purple flowers lie scattered on the ground below. I embrace the relaxed atmosphere.

We travel by jet ski, speeding across the bay to explore the islands. Michael and I journey across to North Stradbroke Island and several smaller islands. When we approach one island we are greeted by a very friendly dolphin who plays around our ski. We sit for a little while with the motor off so we can enjoy this special moment.

A few days into our time away Michael goes fishing, where he meets a massive dugong who swims and plays around him.

We are in paradise. My mind is slowly letting go of everything I no longer want to think about.

At the last minute we issue an invitation to friends to join us for a few days to greet the New Year. We all travel up the coast to one of our favourite holiday locations in Noosa to walk right out to Hells Gate.

After a swim in the ocean and a stroll down the main shopping strip, we relax at one of the many cafés. An interesting fable is shared about a fox carrying a chicken in his mouth. The fox is surprised to see another chicken that looks bigger than the one he is holding, so he lets go of the one he has already caught. Then he realises it is the same chicken – he has seen his own reflection in the water. In grasping for more, he ends up losing what he was already holding.

The moral I draw from this fable is the need to be grateful for what you already have. If you sacrifice what you have, you may lose it all.

New Year's Eve is a special time. For me it has always been a time of gratitude for all that the previous year has gifted, motivating me to determine my dreams and wishes for the coming year. I believe such dreams should be held with the gravity they deserve.

After our friends return home, just Michael and I remain. These last few days are blessed by the magic of togetherness, love and calm.

CHAPTER 1

Finding Magic

For our final full day in the Moreton Bay area, Michael and I decide to take the long windy road up to the Hinterland in Queensland. The road takes many twists and turns. Around every corner I feel drawn closer to the beautiful powerful energy of the 'Fig Tree Walk'.

Even though we've been staying on the coastline of Moreton Bay, overlooking the ocean and surrounding islands, I have found very few thriving Moreton Bay trees in the area. I know that many of the trees I saw on North Stradbroke Island had witnessed much sadness. I am on the outlook to find a tree that will bring more magic into my life.

I recall discovering a Moreton Bay Fig in Perth a few years ago when I stayed with a girlfriend. As soon as I sat at the many feet of this King, I instantly felt honoured. Regal in nature, he welcomed me as I soaked in his long history and grandeur. Old, gentle and enchanting – he enveloped me into the magic of time itself. His woven root system shared earth's journey in contrast with the massive branches covered with foliage that plugged into the heavens above.

I discovered that he was the gateway tree between heaven and earth. Immediately I felt like closing my eyes and feeling the ground beneath me through my own feet. In contrast, my head was in a meditative state that escorted me into a blissful realm. I allowed my mind to drift into all my hopes, dreams and possibilities, and was shown my dreams as if they had already been granted.

Now, in the Hinterland of Queensland, we arrive at the Fig Tree Walk and notice an elevated timber walkway that shows the path ahead. To my surprise a beautiful spirit-woman called Moira stands waiting for me. I've not met Moira before, yet there's a sense of knowing and familiarity about her. She's an old spirit who resides in this special place. Moira looks to be around 90 years of age; she appears frail yet strong. Her dark skin and appearance give away her aboriginal decent. She mutters in her native tongue as she pats my chest and then her own, indicating heart connection. Leading me along the timber walkway I stand in awe as I meet my new friend. There before me is a massive Moreton Bay Fig. Reaching up high, I struggle to see the far-reaching branches. The size of the trunk is many metres wide. Huge leg roots stand like large walls, fanning out and firmly holding the ground. They are massive, majestic and grand.

I'm unsure how I know the spirit lady's name, but Moira takes me in between two of the large root walls. She turns me around, then my back is placed up against the trunk. Moira taps my chest again. I think she knows how I connect into trees. I take my three big breaths, a connection language that allows the truth of tree and human to be felt, experienced and heard.

"Hello," I whisper to this Moreton Bay Fig, while smiling at Moira. Moira grins toothlessly back at me. Her eyes glisten as sunlight catches her spirit. My back is warm. I feel like I am standing inside this Moreton Bay Fig. I feel this to be a sacred space so I show respect. Moira looks up above my head, right up into the massive canopy above me. I cannot help but copy her. When I look back down she is gone, even though I still feel her around me. I blink and wipe my eyes – yet still Moira is not visible. Deep in the crevice of Moreton Bay Fig, I relax. I know I've been brought here on purpose. I wonder if this tree is the same as the one I met in Perth – a tree of dreaming.

"Thank you for coming so far." The words are spoken in a mature female voice.

"I heard you calling and couldn't resist the adventure you offered," I say.

"My magic, your magic… together a dream," the tree continues.

"What happened to the old spirit lady who greeted me?" I ask.

"She is here, but just out of view," comes the reply.

"You hold such a mystical energy," I say, as the hairs on my arms stand on end. My head tingles, yet I feel completely relaxed. I feel in a trance meditative state and decide to sit down. I see magical swirls twisting and spinning, capturing me and drawing me closer. Sitting at the many feet of this Moreton Bay Fig I soak in the gentle and enchanting atmosphere. She envelops me into the magic of time itself. Just like the previous Moreton Bay Fig her woven root system sits above the earth. She too feels like a gateway between heaven and earth. Immediately I feel like closing my eyes and feeling the heartbeat of the ground beneath me through my own feet.

CHAPTER 2

Heart's Connection

Many massive root feet spread out and hold firm to Mother Earth. As I sit, I am swept into a void that draws me again upward. Taking three big breaths into my heart I feel my mind cautioned to quietness. My heart is open to a new conversation.

"Hello." I feel a very different energy around this magnificent Moreton Bay Fig.

"Welcome back into my magic," she continues. "I wondered when you would return. Have you ever met someone and already felt a knowing?" she asks me. "Do you feel this about me now?"

"Yes, I guess so. I do feel comfortable here. I feel 'magic' as well," I comment as my skin tingles slightly.

"Keep your eyes closed – I want to show you something," Moreton Bay Fig requests.

Doing as I'm instructed, I instantly experience colour, at first a little like a kaleidoscope. Patterns and swirls soon turn to faces. There are smiles on faces from different countries. If I look at someone long enough, I can see into their lives; lives of diverse culture. The people bearing faces live in grass huts, brick multi-storey buildings, mudbrick homes and many other kinds of dwellings... my head feels like it is spinning from the quick world trip of diversity, colour and environment. All the faces look back at me, and our eyes lock into a common thread of kindness.

Soon the faces fade, but the intoxication of love lingers. I open my eyes.

"That was a beautiful experience," I say.

"Connection. All connected through a thread of being human," Moreton Bay Fig responds.

"So beautiful. Thank you for sharing," I say quietly. "I felt so much love in the eyes you showed me. Why are you talking with me about this connection? Are trees like this also?" I ask.

"Connections above, below and beyond. Yes, trees too form a special network, just as humans do. A feeling, a hunch and a premonition are always nudging to flow with the pulse of earth. You feel my beat. You see connections, regardless of culture. Our conversation is only possible now because of connection. A beat, a rhythm, a knowing, my friend. Being part of something bigger. The beat is the heart. Your heart, my heart and all the hearts that connect, here now and far away," Moreton Bay Fig continues.

I feel an instant sense of belonging. "Never alone and always connected," I muse.

I take three further breaths into my heart, my platform of connection to the world's hearts and my special connection to my new friend Moreton Bay Fig. I wonder if it is as simple as this – just knowing that there is a worldwide connection in heartbeats. This is how humans and even trees connect globally. I feel calm yet excited about my connection to Moreton Bay Fig.

"Before you leave today, please walk around this entire area," Moreton Bay Fig invites me.

Following a black butterfly with white spots on each wing, I'm taken deeper into the vine-hanging rainforest surrounding my friend.

I approach a second massive ancient Moreton Bay Fig in this area and marvel at his size. I feel this Moreton Bay Fig is male. He is also kind, just like the other. Perhaps they both guard this special sacred space together.

I climb down from the timber walkway and up onto the massive mound where this other Moreton Bay Fig's root system twists around the area. The embankment hangs with massive roots. I look very tiny compared with this giant!

I feel calm, relaxed and excited. I know that an awesome journey awaits, now that I have a heart connection.

CHAPTER 3

Dreaming

After connecting with Moreton Bay Fig, I find that I sleep soundly. I dream for most of the night. I haven't dreamed this vividly in a long time. In my dreaming, I meet old friends. It feels like it used to when we spent time together years before. In this dream space we talk about real life and what is happening now. Even though I busily dream for most of the night, I wake feeling rested. I feel there's an awakening in my dreaming.

I cannot wait to sit by my friend today, and I wonder if Moira will also be there. I wonder if perhaps Moira is the guardian of the land around my new friend, Moreton Bay Fig.

Taking three breaths into my heart, I see flowers in my hand. These are a gift for my new friend. I feel deep gratitude for the vibrant dreams I've started to experience. My bouquet bursts with bright red flowers of the Illawarra flame trees, as well as the deep purple flowers from Jacaranda.

My eyes search for Moira and I notice she's sitting off to the side. When she notices me, she responds with a big wave. At the base of Moreton Bay Fig I place my gift of flowers. Then I sit and look toward my friend.

"Please accept these flowers as a mark of my gratitude today for having reignited my dreams. It's been a long time since I dreamed as I did last night. I love catching up with old friends in vibrant hues of colour and happiness," I thank my friend.

"Good morning to you. I felt it had been too long since you've travelled in your dreams to meet with friends. Your heart was the guide as to where you would go."

I smile as I hear my friend speak.

"Sleep is not just for the exhausted. It is a special time for you to dream beyond," Moreton Bay Fig tells me, her voice motherly. "Too busy in person to stay connected but at night, time and space aren't the same as during waking hours. You also managed to feel and love those no longer living."

"Yes, I did… can you also see my dreams?" I ask.

"I am the tree that sees your hopes and dreams. I help you manifest, revisit and reconnect the threads that enrich your life. You really connected last night, just as we are connecting now. Also, I love the gift of these beautiful flowers," Moreton Bay Fig says, softly and sweetly.

I place both my hands in a prayerful position in front of my heart. I'm immersed in a beautiful feeling of calm. I enjoyed every part of my adventure last night. I loved catching up with people who were difficult to visit during the everyday. Time and space restrict me when I'm awake. I'm excited to discover all this extra time while I sleep to make these connections possible. I've always believed that when a dream is in vivid colour, I am actually visiting the magical soul space.

"Yes, my friend, everyone you saw and spoke with last night remembers the same dream."

"That makes me very happy. It was good to be beside my friend who has been through so much these past couple of years. We lay beside each other and she could share her pain with me. I also saw she was doing OK. That was a gift," I confirm.

"Tonight, just before you sleep, please ask where you want to go and who else you would like to have with you," Moreton Bay Fig suggests.

"Thank you, I'm very excited about nightfall," I reply, then continue, "You are different from how I thought you would be. Because the other Moreton Bay Fig I sat with in Perth was male, I presumed you would be also. But you have a nurturing mother feel," I tell my friend. "Your big root sheets remind me of being tucked into bed at night. You wrap your leg roots across me. I feel your unconditional love and care."

I sit for a little while and then ask, "Can I ask why Moira is here too?"

"Moira is here as guardian of all the trees in this area. This sacred space is special. She followed you all around when you first arrived. She saw you connect. She encouraged this connection and invited you right up close within me. When I saw this, I knew your intentions were pure. You were granted full connection."

Moreton Bay Fig pauses before she invites me: "Hang on girl, now it's time for us to dream. I have now ignited the forgotten in you. Take note of your thoughts, desires and feelings from now on," she gently encourages me.

I bow my head with my hands still in prayer position over my heart.

"My dreams, awake and asleep. I love that. Thank you."

I get up and slowly touch my hand on Moreton Bay Fig's large trunk. I wave to Moira who copies my acknowledgment with a bow, her hands also in prayer position.

Tonight I put my intentions into practice. In my dreams, I manifest old forgotten faces so we can chat for a while. I dream beautiful vibrant vivid dreams, gifted with the power of Moreton Bay Fig.

CHAPTER 4

Re-birth

I'm excited and cannot wait to share how magical my days have begun to be. I start to notice the intricate details of clouds above me and the ground I walk on, as dust puffs behind every step. I notice grasses and wildflowers. My vision is sharpened with a heightened clarity and vibrancy.

Moira is just as excited to see me again, as I am to see her. Her toothless smile is contagious. I flash a warm smile back at her. Moira quickly grabs my hand and we almost run together toward Moreton Bay Fig, who appears brighter today as light filters through her large curtain leg roots, and the surrounding branches and foliage. I look at Moira, who looks like she's busting to share something special with me.

Moira pats her hand on one of Moreton Bay Fig's

leg roots, inviting me to sit. I wonder if perhaps I'm the first person to come here in some time. Moira places her hands over my eyes, encouraging me to tune into my inner vision. Although Moreton Bay Fig and I exchange no words, I sense that what I'm about to be shown will be special.

I feel like I'm in a time warp. Instantly I'm in a space of dreaming. I am taken to the same area beside Moreton Bay Fig, but back before my birth on earth.

Before me I see a much younger Moira and a young pregnant woman. Moira encourages the young girl to lie down beside where I am sitting. I see her pregnant belly contort through a series of contractions as Moira wipes her face, holds her hand, and gives love and support. Moira appears to be the midwife. I watch as a newborn baby is birthed into the world. The large leg roots of Moreton Bay Fig serve to hold up the young mother's legs. My friend Moreton Bay Fig is also holding a loving calm energy to welcome in the new life.

Tears stream down my face. I feel so much love. What a special privileged moment to witness. I wonder how many women have come to birth their babies here.

The tiny baby is held, fed and celebrated.

Moira looks up and makes her way back over to me, pointing toward the very centre of Moreton Bay Fig. I notice an opening in her trunk that I haven't noticed before. It appears big enough for me to enter. Am I still dreaming? Should I enter? Deciding to trust my instincts, I get up and walk inside. Then I'm all alone, except for Moreton Bay Fig.

"Is it OK that I'm in here today?" I ask.

"In here is exactly where you are ready to be. Rest for a moment before I take you somewhere extraordinary. Yes, you are finally ready."

I have no idea where I'm being taken or what I'm about to see or experience. All I know is that I need to trust completely. The space inside Moreton Bay Fig begins to change colour, with swirls of vibrancy. I feel like I'm moving backward in time, very quickly. I see a woman in hospital. Everything is white and very different from the recent birthing experience within nature that I have just witnessed. I sense I'm about to see another birth. I try to move closer to see why I've been bought here. Then I notice that the woman giving birth is my mother. She pushes hard. A doctor and nurse check all her vital statistics as sweat pours from her convulsing body. I continue to watch on as a baby's head crowns. After a few more pushes, helped by the strong contractions, the fragile baby is forced out. Immediately the baby is whisked away. There is not even time for me to have a good look at the baby before it's taken, washed and wrapped. Then I see her returned, all clean.

Finally I see that the baby is me.

I cry again. A tiny pink girl. The little dimple in my cheek is already pressed in place. I'm hungry and tired. Overcome with love for this tiny treasure who is me, tears flow freely. I witness myself, pure and untouched, before life began shaping and changing me.

I close my eyes. Moments later, I find myself back in the core of Moreton Bay Fig.

CHAPTER 5

My Essence of Healing

When I finally calm down emotionally after experiencing my own re-birth, I say, "That was incredible. What a gift to see myself as a tiny, freshly-born baby. Thank you."

"We haven't finished. I want you to take the essence of yourself as a newborn and hold that essence through every fearful event of your life. This is a lightning speed thing to do – you need to continue to trust," Moreton Bay Fig requests of me.

I hold the beautiful delicate baby-essence of myself and see sparks of moments scattered throughout my 50 years of living.

"Now I want you to do the same thing, but this time take your essence through every experience that left you feeling emotional and physical pain."

Once again snapshots of moments flash by very quickly. Fireworks explode through my life, removing all pain. I blink my eyes and wipe my face as I try to take in this vivid dream of me.

"There are many times when you felt you weren't enough, you were lost and didn't belong. The pain of all those times can only be dissolved through holding this true essence of you."

Now I feel like waters are flooding through my life. Rather than drowning, I feel revived, renewed and alive.

Sitting in the core of Moreton Bay Fig I feel just like the tiny baby version of myself – I'm completely exhausted. The core of Moreton Bay Fig darkens, but I don't feel afraid. Rather, I feel safe and loved.

Moira re-appears with her beautiful smile, glowing and lighting everything up. Holding my hand, she returns outside with me. It's so bright out here that I need to cover my eyes. It occurs to me that this would be similar to the startling brightness a newborn experiences after being birthed from the dark holding place of her mother's womb. Moira cannot hold back her excitement and gives me a big motherly hug.

"Was that a journey of my own re-birth?" I turn and ask Moreton Bay Fig.

"How do you feel?" Moreton Bay Fig then asks.

"I feel lighter, free and brand new." I respond.

"You have been granted what you have dreamed. You wanted to be brand new and to finally close the chapter on all that changed you and stole your essence. It is done!"

"I'm speechless. What a privilege to have Moira, who I believe has assisted so many babies in coming into this world."

I feel humbled. The beautiful spirit-woman Moira still holds my hand. My dream is now my reality. I guess I wasn't ready until now. Now I squeeze her hand with one hand. With the other hand, I hold Moreton Bay Fig tightly. We stay like this for quite a while – I don't want to break the magic of this moment. I stand, holding both my midwives tightly.

Eventually I fall asleep. When I wake, I find myself comfortably tucked up in my bed. I feel loved.

I am love.

CHAPTER 6

A Wish

I arrive at the foot of Moreton Bay Fig but I cannot see Moira anywhere. I find this strange, but wonder whether perhaps she now feels comfortable letting me be with Moreton Bay Fig any time, without needing to be present herself.

"Hello," I say as I sit with my back leaning against my friend. "Moira isn't here today?"

"She's no longer needed. Her job was completed yesterday," Moreton Bay Fig replies.

"Was she here for me? I thought all this time she was here for you?" I ask.

"All along she was here for you. She was gifted from this area, from me, to be there for you whenever you were ready."

I felt honoured and a little embarrassed, but very grateful for such a special moment.

"As soon as I met you, my dreaming was heightened. Do you help dreams come true?" I ask.

"Do you have special dreams you would like me to assist you in bringing into being?"

"Being the start of a new year, I always love to think of the things I wish to accomplish. Shall I tell you these?" I ask.

"I know your dreams – you don't need to say them aloud. Sometimes by telling others you dilute the power of your dreams," Moreton Bay Fig tells me.

In my mind's eye, I peruse my dreams. I smile, knowing my friend can also see them. Moreton Bay Fig is my tree-friend, one who can help me plant dream seeds and then watch them manifest and grow.

I find it interesting that Moreton Bay Fig has cautioned me to not tell others my dreams. Often I tell people my dreams, and then I find the dreams fizzle out. Have I been diluting the power of my dreams? In my heart I hold the dreams of the year ahead. I imagine them all coming true. I decide to trust, letting the magic of my tree-friend grow these dreams into reality.

"Thank you," I say.

"You're welcome. Never stop dreaming. Not just in your mind, but also with and through your heart," Moreton Bay Fig replies.

I hold my hand over my heart, and vow to continue to dream big dreams.

It's now dusk and all is quiet. I hear soothing sounds of the flowing water in the nearby stream. Birds sing out, their final song before settling in for the night. I would usually find nightfall eerie and would avoid sitting alone at this time of evening. I guess I'm not really alone when I am sitting beside my large tree-friend. Not far from where she stands, towers the other massive Moreton Bay Fig. I do feel safe; I really do. I have often feared that someone is watching me or waiting to hurt me. But my Moreton Bay Fig tree-friends have now created a very powerful sense of safety that resides deep in the pit of my belonging.

"I feel so serene sitting by you this evening," I whisper.

"You are, just as I am, always. Is this not a common feeling for you?" Moreton Bay Fig asks.

"Yes, I usually feel hypervigilant about every possible danger. I've learned this through my experiences of being pounced on, taken from and hurt as a child."

I hang my head. I don't want to talk of these times, and hope our conversation isn't heading there.

"Sshhh... no longer," Moreton Bay Fig says.

She hears me. I'm relieved to be given permission to allow silence to settle on a chapter I have finally closed. This has been a large area of my life from which I have really craved complete release. Surprisingly, tears spill from my eyes. It is over! As night falls, I see twinkling stars glistening, one by one, in the dark ink sky. The moon is waning so only a slither can be seen.

"Do you wish upon stars as they shoot across the night sky?" Moreton Bay Fig whispers.

"Yes, always. At our farm I often spend time looking up. Without city lights dulling the stars, they shine vibrantly, just like they do here. I always have a wish and dream," I share.

"Without a dream or wish, you would be without the magic."

I'm a little unsure what my friend means.

"Does the magic come from the dream or from the wish? Or is it just magical to aim for things?"

"Without something to dream about, you would be aimless and lost. You would become bored, lazy and unmotivated. As soon as you envisage your dreams, everything around you comes to life to support you."

She is right. I remember visualising a little room at the farm where I could spread out my art, somewhere to sit and ponder. Only days after I had this dream, Michael received a phone call letting him know that four large windows had been ordered the wrong size by a Project Manager at his work. In disbelief, Michael told me the 'wrong' windows were the exact size of the openings upstairs on our back veranda, just out from our bedroom. They were also painted the same colour as our outside house trim! Very soon I was unexpectedly provided with my dream room. It all started with my wish, dream and visualisation – then the reality was manifested.

"I see the answered dreams, as you do. You understand the power of this. It is also very important to really want what you ask for," Moreton Bay Fig cautions.

I laugh because when my youngest son was about four he had successfully ridden a two-wheeler bike for the first time. I'd asked him, if Santa could bring him anything at all, what it would be. Surprisingly, he responded, 'horse poo.' We all laughed, and I remember his shock when he received his wish in pretty wrapping paper under the Christmas tree!

"With all your heart, what do you wish for more than anything? But please – only hold this in your heart," Moreton Bay Fig says.

My wishes are held within my heart. Looking up, a vibrant star shoots across the night sky. A tear trickles down my cheek. In my heart I hold completeness, and a body free from what has held it for so long. I hold a heart, free to love and be loved. I imagine feeling happy, laughing and attracting happiness in many forms. I notice all the good in the world. I am connected to all that brings me worthiness. I eat, sleep and move with grace. I am healed, healthy and I embody all I should have always been. I am able to gently reach my hand out to others because I am ready to help. My writing, dreaming and unique gifts are honoured, and I belong. People will seek special connections to nature, they will awaken as well to the gifts shared through my writing and public speaking, and they will give back.

I sit in silence. My friend Moreton Bay Fig has heard my heart's dreams and wishes. She is part of the process of manifestation.

My heart tonight is full. I already feel all that I wish and long for.

CHAPTER 7

Transparency of Thought

The sun casts pink and red hues across the setting sky. Night can be a fearful time of day but beside my new friend, the massive Moreton Bay Fig, I feel comforted. I lie on Mother Earth and rest my head on one of her large root legs above-ground. My eyes gaze upward. At first I can still make out the detail and shape of her massive leaves – then, like a shadow or silhouette, I see only light and dark. Stars glisten and twinkle, inviting a big beautiful moon. By moonlight I take my heart connection breaths.

"Good evening, my giant tree-friend."

I smile and settle in her magic. "May I know and call you by name?" I ask.

"My name is Jamiah, which means 'beautiful, kind, good, passionate, sweet, loving and holding the ability to rise above'. I invite and invoke dreaming for anyone who takes rests under me. Are you ready to go?" she invites me.

Closing my eyes, I see kaleidoscope swirls of colour. This isn't the first time I have experienced so much colour around my friend Moreton Bay Fig. I feel a familiar sense of spinning as I'm taken up once more. In dreaming, I'm taken into a vortex beyond the here and now. I'm shown a mid-centre void. On my own body I'm shown that my heart holds the key of entry to the place I'm invited to visit. I'm taken to a place of no speaking as we know it, a place where no words are used. Rather, thoughts are transparent and shared by all. I have dreamed of this place before. Walking past people on a path I hear in my own mind the thoughts of those I pass; I hear comments of praise for the colour, vibrancy and beauty. It is so stunning, and I too share my wonder. I notice there is no time or space for anything negative, but only happiness, calm and belonging. Feelings are heightened. It is like my own gratitude has been amplified, and I witness a world without anger, pain or concern.

I don't want to leave. Sitting down at the edge of a vast clearing, I look over mountains as far as the eye can see, as well as animals, people and nature abundant with trees, flowers and greenery. I walk past a large lake where swans glide across the water. This is paradise; some sort of utopia – heaven on earth. As I pass, I hear people's thoughts as they admire the beauty of the area and the perfect weather. I imagine they must also hear my thoughts of amazement and wonder. I decide to lie down on a grassy bank beside the nearby lake. I close my eyes and feel the grass beneath my body.

I drift off to sleep. When I stir slightly, I hear Moreton Bay Fig speaking: "Welcome back to your reality."

"It's usually good to be back. However I actually preferred where you took me just then," I reply, as I realise I'm back at the base of my friend Moreton Bay Fig, Jamiah. "Life is not as translucent and filled with gratitude here. Rather, most people have glasses covering their sad eyes, shields to ward off confusion and costumes to hide their real selves. I believe this isn't usually intentional, but rather a way humans have been trained, to try to fit in and belong."

Then, sitting up with my hand on Jamiah's smooth bark, I ask, "How can habits of worry, comparison and negativity be broken?"

"Only you can make these changes in your life. Like a magnet, the universe will draw to you those people, events and situations that hold the same vibration as you. And as with a magnet, you can repel those stuck in their negativity. Try experimenting with this tomorrow. Consciously keep your thoughts clear and grateful. Observe those who are drawn to you and those who cannot come too close."

It sounds worth exploring. I am keen to shift my own negative self-sabotage that attracts others stuck in the same traps.

"Thank you, Jamiah, for the dreaming, and for allowing me time and space within your magic. I will let you know how I go," I promise.

I wish my beautiful Moreton Bay Fig, Jamiah, stood outside my back door, so I could sit here more often. I know I only have limited time to dream a little and unlock my new understanding.

CHAPTER 8

Changing Old Habits

I walk up to Moreton Bay Fig today and feel incredibly mindful. Actually, since I first connected into this massive majestic tree, my life has slowed to a comfortable steady pace. Usually I do the opposite of this – I rush, trying to do many things at once and I am often left feeling stressed and worried that I've forgotten something.

However, now I feel calm and more relaxed.

"Morning," I say.

"Good to see you are becoming more in sync with the natural rhythm of life," Jamiah responds.

"Since meeting you, and particularly since I went back to my beginning, my own re-birth, I feel very settled. I am enjoying taking my time to make decisions about what I'm doing, while I wash dishes and purchase food to cook," I am proud to tell my friend.

"There has been a re-setting, an elimination of the programmed ways you've been before now. Yes, you should feel this and notice how it affects every part of your day."

"I've noticed my conversations are more focussed and natural. I feel less quick to blurt things out, rather just enjoying what is being said by others. I'm able to listen more and turn off my own inner chatter. The biggest change I've noticed, however, is not trying to escape through shoving food in my mouth to fill the empty void inside."

I feel shocked now as I really consider how I have been experiencing life.

"Now the real work can begin to get you back on track with your own optimal way of being."

So much had already been done and I can't imagine what more could be done!

"What do I need to do, or not do? I'm unsure what you mean," I reply honestly.

"Start each day with your feet firmly on the

ground. Not in shoes, but bare feet. I want you to imagine every ache, pain or destructive feeling – anything at all that isn't helping you. Then feel the earth drawing these things out of you, through your feet. Stand on your toes three times while taking three big breaths at the same time. Then wipe your feet across the earth. Each day you will notice a huge difference in the way you feel, particularly in your body. Become mindful about your body, thoughts and emotions," Moreton Bay Fig says.

I know I can commit to this practice and I am keen to experience the changes.

Today it is still. I hear birds in the surrounding trees around my friend. They also appear happy and unrushed.

I welcome my calmer state.

CHAPTER 9

Accepting Authenticity

I walk up to Jamiah today and cannot resist reaching out to touch her smooth textured bark. Every tree is different in appearance – like fingerprints, no two trees are the same. There are textured layers of growth, as well as the odd patch that looks like a cut that has opened her up – her scars of yesterday.

"Good morning," I say, after a short while. "When I meet a special tree like you I always discover something about myself. You reflect back something unique to me. Today I cannot stop admiring your bark, the outer casing that the world sees," I share my observation.

Moreton Bay Fig returns her own observations: "I notice your own skin is lightly freckled. You are casual in appearance, which is inviting. Your messy hair shows me you like to look a little carefree."

I smile, exposing my dimple. Jamiah adds, "Extra happiness in your face."

"I used to fuss and worry so much about how others saw me. As I've grown older and learned to relax, I have noticed I'm now more approachable. When I have fussed about looking polished, I have not been as approachable," I reflect back.

"Yes, correct. Being relaxed and natural is what draws people toward you. More people should be aware of this magic."

I rest my back against one of her large leg roots and am once more taken inward. I'm taken to the core of what my exterior displays. I notice I'm not so casual and I hear echoes of all I imagine others to think and feel when they are around me. I have many varied outlooks, ideas and ways of being. My uniqueness can often come under the fire of those who have no understanding of who I really am. I believe my own exterior can lead others to draw incomplete or false conclusions as to who I am. In fact, I know I can portray my external appearance in many different ways, producing various personas or versions of myself for others.

My thoughts take me to the external façade I learned to wear as a child. My mask was one of being OK, even though I wasn't OK at all at times. As an adult I still smile even though all I really want to do is cry for the ways others misunderstand who I really am.

"My friend Jamiah, the way I feel is not always what I portray. I hold fear around the ways I am misunderstood. I know it's because some people have no understanding in their own lives of some of the things to which I've been exposed or have experienced," I explain.

I wondered if any wisdom or a gift from Jamiah might help me out.

"I am different, which I cannot hide. What you see is what you get," Jamiah, Moreton Bay Fig, says. "Many people visit me daily because of this difference. In life as a human you move around and mix with many types of people. Judgements always hold a mirror up to those who make the judgements. Learn to feel sorry for the person who judges, for they are really judging themselves."

I have heard this before but right now I find no comfort knowing that someone judging me just doesn't accept something in themselves, or their own limited life hasn't yet exposed them to a certain understanding. Perhaps they have developed a fear about something unknown, or even about something too intimately known.

My thoughts are interrupted.

"It is never your job to change other people's minds; to teach, explain, or act a certain way for their comfort. It is a strong person who can just be themselves without any agenda. Just be you, Rochelle. When you compromise your own truth, you slip into being inauthentic. Spend more time getting to know who you are. Learn your own likes and dislikes and allow others the same privilege."

Jamiah pauses before continuing, "Gift yourself the acceptance that you aren't meant to understand everyone, just as they may not understand you. Know that it doesn't matter what others think."

I have to interrupt: "I am challenged by this. Imagine if someone didn't like how you looked and they cut you down. I feel cut down at times by the opinions of others."

As I say this, I feel sadness.

"This cannot be helped. All I can do is be the true

version of myself. This is also all you can do," I'm told.

Throughout history, people have been ridiculed just for their skin colour, sexual preference or other differences from the dominant social group. I feel sadness for those who have been harmed, mocked or even killed just for being who they are. It's all very well just being who I am. It's all very well saying that it's the judgemental, opinionated person who has the problem. But I don't see any solution here. I feel confused and even annoyed by the tendency of people to not allow others to be freely themselves.

"I can allow everyone to be who they choose to be. But what can I do about those who don't allow this in me or others?" I ask.

"Not a thing. Accept they don't have understanding, insight or enough love in their hearts for other people's differences. If you try to change other people, you are no different from them. Acceptance is the key. Accept those you see as ignorant, judgmental and intolerant. If you don't give energy to your own annoyance, you will be free to just be the person you're meant to be."

She is right. I'm interested to see how making a conscious effort to accept differences of opinion will set me free.

"Thank you," I stand and face my friend. "I see you and I admire your differences."

"I also see you and love everything about you," Jamiah concludes.

CHAPTER 10

The Magic of In-Between

There's that space between here and there. In my own existence there's a moment between what is and what could be. Sometimes I get a feeling, a knowing, a sense of déjà vu in seemingly new places. I can feel bewildered or have complete clarity. This is the moment, the in-between place.

I breathe through my heart and connect to all of those places where I feel and experience complete clarity between the mystical dream space. Each moment feels like a veil separating the two. I feel I'm right in the middle here by my friend Moreton Bay Fig. No other tree has me suspended between two worlds, feelings or states of being. I am in that moment, in between really wanting something with all my heart, and gaining what I want, the moment when thoughts become reality.

"Your mind, your dreaming and your reality are very heightened today," Moreton Bay Fig states.

Her words wake me up from my day-dreaming. I snap back into the here and now.

"Yes, everything seems brightened somehow. I have clarity, yet everything is also hazy," I reply. "It's like I'm drifting off to sleep and just about to launch into that place of dreaming. I'm awake, yet experiencing a daydream. I feel in between thinking something and doing it, sitting in a pause between it all," I try to explain.

"Many don't glimpse much of the sliver of magic called the 'in-between'. In that moment you can go in any direction, wishing it or seeing it come to fruition. Don't leave this moment too soon," Moreton Bay Fig says.

So, I don't. I feel the anticipation of the 'in-between'. I feel its vastness. Without limits in any direction I believe that everything and anything is possible. A thought is but a single droplet in a vast body of water, but it can cast wide ripples. An idea can expand into a breakthrough that changes everything for good.

In this moment, as the droplet is poised to

fall, time stands still. I've stumbled into part of the essence of my friend Moreton Bay Fig called Jamiah and every massive member of her family – the essence that bridges what is with what could be. I breathe in and out, pausing in the in-between spaces, the 'now' moments.

"I have so many dreams I wish to become reality. This very space I experience right here and now is the magic, isn't it? It's the magic that launches its reality?" I ask.

"Indeed, my friend, it is. How do you feel suspended between the dream and the reality?" I'm then asked.

"It feels like I'm in a big translucent bubble that is floating upwards. One moment I'm just floating and then my bubble is popped. Everything becomes something different," I try to explain. "Is this the same for everyone?"

"All dreams are unique. Your desire, state of mind and feelings are all special to you. What's important is knowing the moment that exists between it all. Magic is felt in the moments when dreams are possibilities."

I smile as I think about the gap between what is

and could be. I'm not meant to figure anything out. I'm meant to feel suspended, held in the magic of not pinning it down.

I feel I've stumbled into all that exists in the 'essence' of my friend.

CHAPTER 11

Imagination

I find myself resting by the outer above-ground leg roots of Moreton Bay Fig, reaching far away. Some distance away from the main trunk of my friend, beautiful patterned fingertips reach out across Mother Earth. These roots hold firm and also soak up all the nutrients to sustain the growth of this majestic ancient.

I find myself playing as I did as a child. My finger traces patterns and swirls in the dirt. I imagine that the dirt becomes a blackboard for me to firstly draw simple images. As a child I loved to draw trees, their trunks, branches and leaves. Then I would wipe the dirt-board clean to draw birds, dogs and other animals. I enjoy recapturing my childhood sense of freedom to draw whatever I wish.

"Imagination," I hear the sweet voice of Jamiah.

"Where do the ideas all come from?" I ask.

"Your subconscious feeds your imagination. Sometimes these thoughts are buried deep within. Perhaps you saw, heard and experienced something, or a spark of something, completely new. Your imagination can come alive in a picture, a piece of writing or just a dream. I love to help amplify imagination in humans," Moreton Bay Fig says.

I smile as I think of being like a child on a wild adventure, believing everything is possible. I can fly in my dreams and allow my imagination to take me anywhere. Toward the unknown I can venture, without the fear of failure. Imagination is my ticket to experience anything I wish for.

"What happens as we grow? As I have aged, my imagination has shrunk."

"Reality restricts imagination. Yet all things are still made possible through imagination. If anything were possible, what would you imagine?" Jamiah asks me.

"I would first imagine a world with more kindness, and with less greed and self-absorption," I respond.

"If everyone had the same imagined wish, then

that is how the world would be," Jamiah says.

I guess it would. Kindness – global kindness – would be such a powerful imagined way to be.

I continue to play in the dust with my finger and draw a smiley face. Around this I draw the world and big beams of happiness surrounding it all. Just imagining this makes me feel as if it's already so.

"I cannot even begin to know a world without imagination. As a child the world was a free space to play in and escape to. Imagination became my opportunity to be anything I wanted to be," I say.

"Today you remember the importance of this gift of imagination. Playing here also re-gifts you your youth," Moreton Bay Fig shares.

"I want more of this!" I laugh.

I immediately think of the Adventures of Peter Pan, Tinkerbell and the other fairy tales told to me as a child. This kind of imagination births great movies, inspiring songs and vivid images. How important the imagination is, and what colour and vibrancy it brings!

"I pledge to treasure and dedicate more time to just imagining," I say.

"Remember to visit anytime you need your imagination heightened."

"I will," I promise.

I am in no hurry and continue to draw in the dust around my friend. In my heart, I know this is not the last time I will visit her.

Jamiah Moreton Bay Fig has gifted me the freedom to dream once more. With a re-birth essence of self I have been taught how to cleanse and heal parts of my life. She has held such a magical space where I can dream anew. I can hold dreams in my heart which will then be manifested in reality.

I feel like I had to earn the right to meet this majestic tree. With honour and gratitude, I'm so glad I took the journey.

Also by Rochelle

Banyan Tree Wisdom: My Gift to You
Banyan Tree Wisdom: Wisdom Cards
Meeting Rosie Banyan:
Learning Forgiveness, Trust and Love
I Give You My Word: Journal

EARTH GIANT TREE GIFT SERIES
(GIFT BOOKS & AUDIO BOOKS)

Book 1: Oak Tree's Gift
Book 2: Baobab Tree's Gift
Book 3: Banyan Tree's Gift
Book 4: Rainbow Gum's Gift
Book 5: Olive Tree's Gift
Book 6: Pagoda Tree's Gift
Book 7: Snow Gum Tree's Gift
Book 8: Moreton Bay Fig's Gift

ALCHEMY OILS

Banyan Tree: 'Restore Balance', 'Dream',
'Release' & 'Beauty Wisdom Power'
Oak Tree: 'Truth'
Baobab Tree 'Connection'
Banyan Tree 'Balance'
Rainbow Gum 'Joy'
Olive Tree 'Confidence'
Pagoda Tree 'Clarity'
Snow Gum Tree 'Motivated'
Moreton Bay Fig 'Dreaming'

www.treevoice.global

About the Author

A busy business owner, wife and mother, Rochelle thrived in the corporate and finance world in her early adult years. Then, after her fourth son, a wave of post-natal depression debilitated her, forcing her to re-visit the horrors of her sexually abusive childhood. With grit and determination she laboured against her own broken past and breathed life back into her shutdown heart, cracking open its language and capturing it in writing. She learned to trust in the universal soul path she'd stepped onto.

Each time she experienced a healing method that helped her, Rochelle became qualified in that field to then help others. She became a Bowen Therapist, Reiki and Seichem Master, Clinical Hypnotherapist using NLP methods, Journey Worker and Intuitive Healer. She also owned and ran a Day Spa and Healing Centre in North East Victoria.

Rochelle now immerses herself in connections with nature as they flow, bringing to life the lessons and messages through writing, speaking and facilitating. Her journey has led her to many parts of the globe. She has pitched to Hollywood in New York; she has hosted women's retreats in Bali; she has learned from poverty-stricken leaders in Senegal Africa; and she discovered the 'simple' life in Vanuatu.

Rochelle's message is honest, raw and authentic, and her words are greatly needed as we all navigate our next chapter here on earth.

AUTHOR, SPEAKER, ALCHEMIST,
A LOVER OF NATURE AND
VIBRANT LIVING

Connect with Rochelle

hello@treevoice.global

www.facebook.com/TreeVoiceAuthor

www.facebook.com/RochelleHeverenAuthor

Instagram: @treevoiceglobal

Instagram: @rochelle_with_love_x

www.treevoice.global

www.ingramcontent.com/pod-product-compliance
Lightning Source LLC
Chambersburg PA
CBHW032050290426
44110CB00012B/1026